What's in This Book

If you are asked to picture an animal, what comes to your mind first? A dog? A bird? Perhaps a zebra? Chances are you thought of a vertebrate, an animal with a backbone. But vertebrates, which include the animals we are the most familiar with—mammals, birds, fish, reptiles, and amphibians—actually make up less than 5% of all animal species. All the rest of the animals alive today—more than 95%—are invertebrates, animals without backbones. Can you picture a spotted ladybug, spiny sea urchin, or slimy garden slug? *Animals Without Backbones: Invertebrates* explores the lives of the many fascinating invertebrates that survive and thrive without the need for a backbone.

The COME LEARN WITH ME series encourages children's natural curiosity about the world by introducing them to exciting areas in science. Each book deals with a specific topic, and can be read alone or together with an adult. With lively, reader-friendly texts and numerous engaging illustrations, the books will entertain and inform children and adults alike. No previous knowledge of the subject is needed. Scientific vocabulary appears in **bold type** and is defined in context, but is also listed in the Glossary at the end of the book. Let these books be your guide as you enter the fascinating world of science, where you are sure to discover many new interests and vastly expand your horizons.

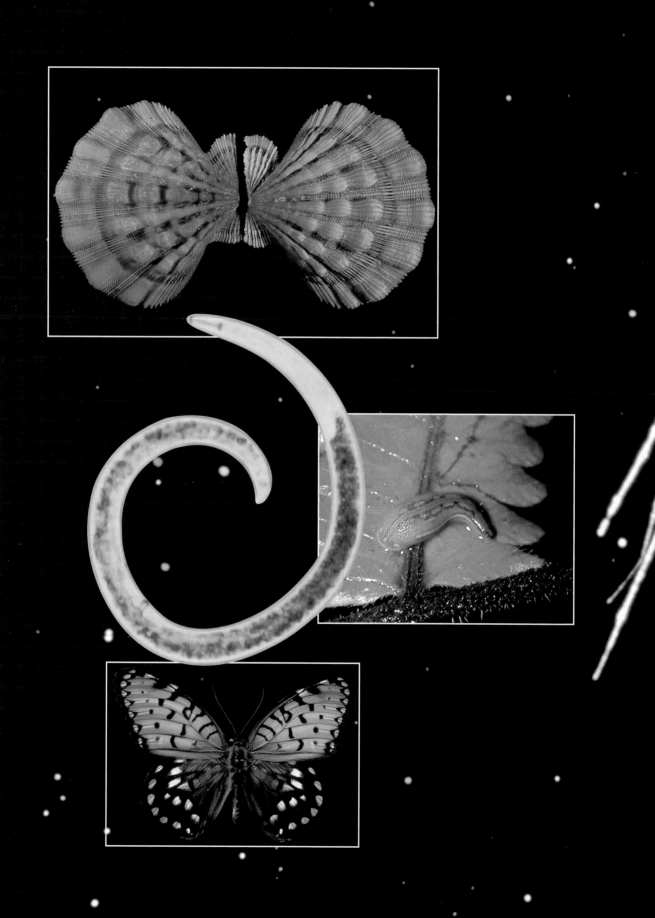

COME LEARN WITH ME

Animals Without Backbones: Invertebrates

Text by Bridget Anderson

BANK STREET COLLEGE OF EDUCATION
in association with the
AMERICAN MUSEUM OF NATURAL HISTORY
for Lickle Publishing Inc

First published in 2003 by

LICKLE PUBLISHING INC

Library of Congress Control Number

2002113573

ISBN: 1-890674-14-1

ILLUSTRATION AND PHOTO CREDITS

American Museum of Natural History 2tl, 2bl, 8l, 9b, 10t, 10tl, 10cl, 10b, 11b, 20bl, 21t, 21b, 25cr, 30, 31t, 31c, 32tr,
34b, 36c, 37b, 38c, 41cr, 41cl— AMNH photographers Matt Cormons 10tr; Enrico Ferorelli 8l; Bruce Hunter 43cr;
B.J. Kaston 6-7, 9cr, 36t, 39t, 39c, 40c, 40b; Josef H. Knull 36b; G. Lower 43cr;Frank Puza 10br, 41b; George Raeihle
8br; J.E. Thompson 38t, 38-39b—; B. Anderson 9t; David Bagby 33cl; Dee Breger, Lamont-Doherty Earth Observatory
41tr; Charles Davey 16t, 17tr (courtesy deep steep, Annie Walker and Renay Arbour); Wim van Egmond 20br, 25tr,
37t; Keith F. Goodnight, Southern Methodist University 11t, 16b, 24b, 29t, 31b, 37t, 43t; National Oceanic and
Atmospheric Administration (NOAA) Photo Library 1, 2-3, 6c, 12, 14b, 19br, 22t, 22c, 23c, 29br, 35tl, 35tr, 40t, 42t,
45cl, 45br—NOAA photographers Henry Ansley 42b; John N. Cobb 17t; Stephen Cook 23t; Kip Evans 18-19, 20tr;
Commander William Harrigan 15b; Mary Hollinger 15t; L. Levin 35b; Photo Collection of Dr. James P. McVey 14t,
22-23b, 43b, 44; William Millhouser 24t; B. Walden 17b—; Peter Mullin c 1999 27tl, c 2000 2cl, 26b, 27tr, 27b;
Mark Siddall 2cr, 29b; University of California Board of Regents, used with permission: Suzanne Paisley 28t, 28c;
John Walker 7r, 10cr, 24cr, 25cl, 25bl, 25br, 32cl, 32bl, 33tr, 33cr, 33bl;
Illustrations: Chris Forsey 13

Series Director: Charles Davey LLC, New York
Text by Bank Street College of Education:
Andrea Perelman, Project Manager; Elisabeth Jakab, Project Editor
Photographs unless otherwise credited from the American Museum of Natural History:
Maron L. Waxman, Editorial Director; Elizabeth Borda, Scientific Consultant
Art Direction, Production & Design: Charles Davey, Charles Davey design LLC
Photo research: Erin Barnett

Printed in China

CONTENTS

Incredible Invertebrates

Imagine life if you didn't have a head. How would you think, see, smell, or eat? Did you know there are many animals that survive and thrive even though they don't have heads? Jellyfish and sea anemones cannot see or smell the way people do.

What if one day, your stomach decided to come out through your mouth and digest your meal while it was still on your plate? Sounds impossible, but that is exactly how many sea stars eat.

Although a jellyfish lacks a head and a brain, it can successfully move, sting, and catch its food.

Imagine if instead of having two legs for walking, you had six, eight, ten, or even a hundred legs like a millipede! How would you coordinate those legs? What if you did not have legs at all, but a foot was attached to your belly? You could only move by lying on your stomach and scrunching and stretching the muscles in your foot. It might sound strange, but that is a normal way of life for snails and slugs.

Most animals, in fact, have lives radically different from our own. Humans are vertebrates, which means we have a backbone and other bones making up our skeleton. Cats, dogs, birds, fish, frogs, even snakes have bony skeletons and are also vertebrates. Most animals, however—more than 95% of all the animals on Earth—do not have backbones. They are the invertebrates.

Left and background images: Spiders called orb weavers make large circular webs to catch their prey.

Animals Everywhere

There are well over a million different kinds of animals living on Earth today—most of them are invertebrates. They live in every place you can think of. Search between blades of grass, under rocks, in tree bark, and among sand grains. You will find thousands of invertebrates crawling, burrowing, flying, and jumping. Look on the sidewalk, and you will see tiny creatures navigating along cracks. And those are just the land invertebrates. Many invertebrates live in water—in oceans, lakes, rivers, and puddles. Anywhere water collects, you are sure to find an invertebrate animal.

Sea anemones live on the ocean floor.

Many invertebrate animals can be found in the moving waters and along the wet banks of streams.

Every kind of animal (both vertebrate and invertebrate) has a unique shape, behavior, and lifestyle, but they all have a few characteristics in common. Animals need to eat food for energy, they can react to their environments by moving or changing shape, and they are able to create new life. Animal bodies are made up of tiny living building blocks called **cells.** Small animals are made of only a few cells, larger animals out of many more. Different kinds of cells have specific jobs to make the body of an animal work. An animal grows by making more cells.

The bones inside the bodies of vertebrate animals give them support and structure. Without your bones, you would be a soft mass of flesh inside your skin. You wouldn't be able to stand up, point your finger, or keep your head from flopping over.

Invertebrates live without bones inside their bodies. They have other ways to give their bodies structure and protection.

Hippopotamuses (top) and other vertebrate animals may be larger and more noticeable, but the most numerous animals on Earth are invertebrates, such as lobsters (middle) and cockroaches (bottom).

Classifying Animals

All animals—from bears to leeches, to butterflies, to parrots—belong to the **animal kingdom**. To keep them all straight, animals are divided into groups, called **phyla** (singular: phylum). The animals in each phylum share a special combination of characteristics that other animals do not have. For example, animals in the phylum Arthropoda have segmented bodies and jointed legs.

While animals in a phylum share a general body plan, there can be many variations of that plan. Therefore, members of a phylum are separated into smaller groups that share more specific traits. Within the phylum Arthropoda, for example, there are insects, millipedes, centipedes, spiders, and crabs, among others.

Insects, millipedes, centipedes, arachnids, and crustaceans are all classified in the phylum Arthropoda. They have segmented bodies, jointed legs, and an exoskeleton.

Animal Species

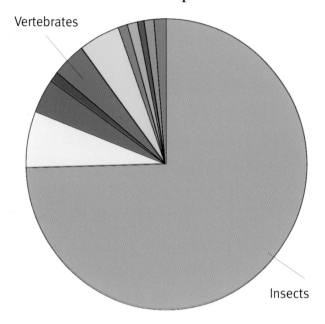

Vertebrates

Insects

Of all the animal species living on Earth today almost 75% are insects (in the phylum Arthropoda). Fewer than 5% of all animal species are vertebrates (in the phylum Chordata).

These groups are then further divided into smaller and smaller groups, each with more characteristics in common. The smallest and most specific groups that animals can be divided into are called **species.**

Members of a species share almost all of the same characteristics— they look and act alike. They can also reproduce to make a new animal of that species. The process of grouping things according to characteristics they share is called **classification.**

Animals have common names that typically describe their appearance. For example, the "moon jelly" is a jellyfish with a white, rounded body that looks like a full moon. But common names change depending on where you live and what language you speak. To avoid confusion, scientists have given each species a unique scientific name in Latin. For example, the scientific name of a moon jelly is *Aurelia aurita.*

Aurelia aurita is called a moon jelly in English because it looks like a full moon.

Animal Family Tree

Animals in the same species are related to one another, like a large extended family. In fact, scientists think that if you go back far enough in Earth's history, all animals are related in some way. Through classification you can trace an animal's lineage, like a family tree, and see how it is related to the rest of the animal kingdom.

In general, animals classified in the same groups are more closely related than those in different groups. Jellyfish and sea anemones are both grouped in the phylum Cnidaria. They are more closely related to each other than to an octopus in the phylum Mollusca.

Background image: A colony of star coral reproduces in the water.

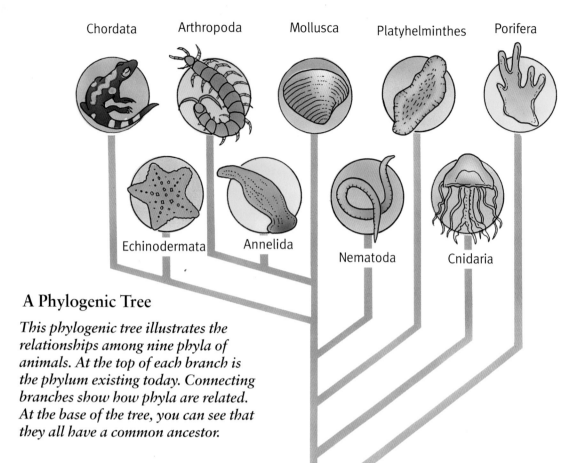

Chordata Arthropoda Mollusca Platyhelminthes Porifera

Echinodermata Annelida Nematoda Cnidaria

Common Ancestor

A Phylogenic Tree

This phylogenic tree illustrates the relationships among nine phyla of animals. At the top of each branch is the phylum existing today. Connecting branches show how phyla are related. At the base of the tree, you can see that they all have a common ancestor.

The most closely related animals are those in the same species. A moon jelly is more closely related to another moon jelly than it is to any other animal, even other kinds of jellyfish.

The relationships between all animals can be illustrated by making a phylogenic tree—a family tree for the animal kingdom. Branches on the tree show how animals are related to each other. Animals on branches far from each other are distantly related. Animals on branches near to each other are more closely related. On the phylogenic tree pictured above, each branch represents one phylum. Where the branches come together, the animals in those phyla have a common ancestor.

There are more than 20 phyla in the animal kingdom, and as scientists continue to discover more animals, this number grows. All vertebrate animals belong to one phylum, Chordata. Invertebrate animals make up all of the other phyla in the animal kingdom. In this book, you will be introduced to eight major phyla of invertebrate animals. You can see the relationships between these phyla on the phylogenic tree above.

Phylum Porifera

sponge

Sponges are grouped in the phylum Porifera. They are the simplest multicellular animals living on Earth today. Scientists think that ancient sponges were some of Earth's first animals.

All sponges live in water— mostly warm ocean water. They exist in many different shapes, sizes, and colors. Some are vase-shaped, others barrel-shaped, and still others take the shape of whatever surface they grow on. Many species form branches like an underwater bush. In fact, for a long time people thought sponges were plants, since they didn't appear to move.

The tiny sponge crab camouflages itself with a sponge on its back.

Scientists now know that although sponges typically stay anchored for most of their lives, they do have the ability to move. Sponge **larvae** (young sponges) swim in the water until they find a place to take anchor and grow.

In addition to producing swimming larvae, sponges can reproduce by a process called **budding**. This means that they can form a new growth on the side of their bodies. Eventually this "bud" breaks off and finds its own place to anchor and grow.

Fish and other aquatic animals make their homes inside vase sponges.

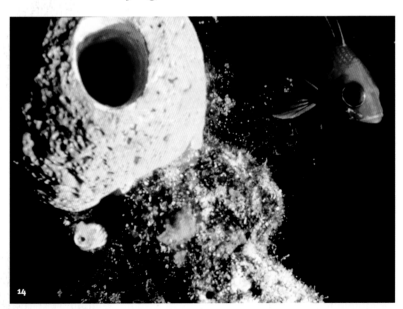

The red beard sponge grows on shells and other surfaces in shallow, sunny waters.

Slowly the cells regroup and start growing together. Eventually they create miniature versions of the original sponge.

Many animals love to eat sponges. Since adult sponges are anchored to one place, they cannot run away from predators. So many sponges produce a toxic chemical that is poisonous to other animals. Even other sponges will choose not to anchor too close to a toxic sponge.

Sponges have the amazing ability to **regenerate**. That is, they can regrow parts of their bodies which have been damaged. If part of a sponge is broken off, the damaged sponge repairs itself, and the piece that broke off grows into a new sponge. Scientists have tested regeneration by separating a sponge into its individual cells and dropping them into a dish of water.

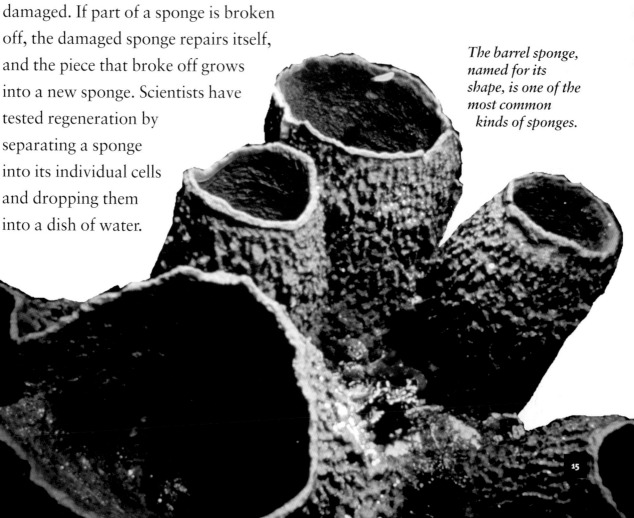

The barrel sponge, named for its shape, is one of the most common kinds of sponges.

Useful Sponges

When you wash dishes or wipe up a spill, you might use a dish cloth, a paper towel, or a sponge. Sponges are especially useful because they absorb liquid through lots of tiny holes. Although most of the sponges you buy today are artificial, the original cleaning sponges were actually the skeletons of sponge animals.

Today, most people use synthetic (artificial) sponges for cleaning.

The phylum name Porifera means "pore-bearers" in Latin. The outer layers of sponges are full of holes, or pores, called **ostia** (singular: ostium). These ostia lead to a system of canals that run through the body of a sponge. Water enters the ostia, flows through the canals of the body, and exits through a larger pore, called an osculum.

Special cells lining the canals of the sponge move the water along using whiplike structures called flagella. Flagella wag back and forth, creating a water current to bring in oxygen and filter tiny organisms and other food particles from the water. They also push carbon dioxide and waste materials out of the body.

Sponge bodies are made up of two layers of cells separated by a jellylike substance. A sponge's skeleton, made of minerals or fibers called **spicules**, grows in this jellylike substance. Some

A Sponge's Body

Water (blue arrows) enters the body of a sponge through tiny holes, the ostia, and exits through a larger hole, the osculum.

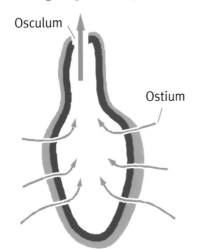

Osculum

Ostium

Close-up of Two Layers of a Sponge's Body

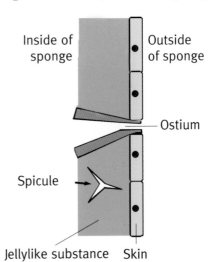

Inside of sponge

Outside of sponge

Ostium

Spicule

Jellylike substance   Skin

A sponge's spicules, the fibers that form its skeleton, grow in the jellylike substance beneath a sponge's skin.

16

Natural sponges are used widely in health spas and are considered excellent for cleaning the body .

After natural sponges are harvested from the ocean, they are laid out in the sun to dry.

sponge skeletons are hard as rock, while others are flexible. Their texture depends on what the spicules are made of. Sponge skeletons made of mineral spicules are rigid and hard. The natural sponges people use for bathing and cleaning have a fine mesh of spicule fibers called **spongin** that can hold a lot of water.

For centuries, people have harvested sponges from the oceans to use for cleaning. They have even created underwater sponge "farms." Sponge divers collect sponges growing on the ocean floor and then lay them out to dry. When dry, the body of a sponge is scrubbed away, leaving just the spongin skeleton.

Sponges live in shallow oceans where they can anchor to rocks on the seafloor.

Phylum Cnidaria

Jellyfish, sea anemones, hydra, and corals are grouped in the phylum Cnidaria, which means "stinging nettles" in Greek. These animals live mostly in oceans with a few species found in rivers and lakes. They can look quite beautiful, with their tentacles gently swaying in the water. All cnidaria have the ability to sting as a defense against predators and to catch food.

Most cnidaria have no eyes and cannot see. Instead, their tentacles sense passers by. When the tentacles touch something, they send out painful, poisonous stinging impulses either to hurt a predator or to stun prey. Tentacles also serve to pull food into the animal's mouth. Once inside the mouth, food is digested in the central cavity, a large saclike space in the body. Cnidaria get rid of waste through the mouth opening as well.

A jellyfish spends most of its life as a medusa floating in the water.

Cnidaria have two main body forms: the **polyp** form that anchors itself in one place, and the **medusa** form that floats freely in the water. Many cnidaria spend part of their lives in each form.

Polyp means "many feet." Sea anemones, hydra, and corals spend most of their lives as polyps attached to a rock, shell, or the sea floor by the bottom part of their bodies.

Their mouths and tentacles are located on top of their tube-shaped bodies.

A jellyfish begins its life as a swimming larva that soon becomes a polyp and anchors itself. The polyp eventually breaks apart into many free-floating medusae. With umbrella-shaped bodies, jellyfish spend their adult lives floating and pulsing in the water.

Scientists think that ancient cnidaria were some of the first animals to develop muscles and nerves— the body tissues that help animals move in reaction to their surroundings. These tissues are very simple in cnidaria, and therefore the movements of cnidaria are simple.

A sea anemone spends most of its life as a polyp anchored to the seafloor.

Jellyfish, Hydra, and Sea Anemones

As long as a bus and as tiny as a fingernail, many species of jellyfish float in the ocean dangling their long, thin tentacles. They carry out mesmerizing dances as their translucent (almost clear) bodies pulse with the water currents and their tentacles sway in response.

But watch your step on the beach. Sometimes jellyfish drift ashore and lie in a jellylike mass among the sand and rocks. While they cannot live out of water, they can still sting! Most jellyfish stings cause little or no discomfort in humans. However, the Portuguese man-o-war, a jellyfish relative, can cause pain that lasts several weeks.

Hydras, the smallest kind of

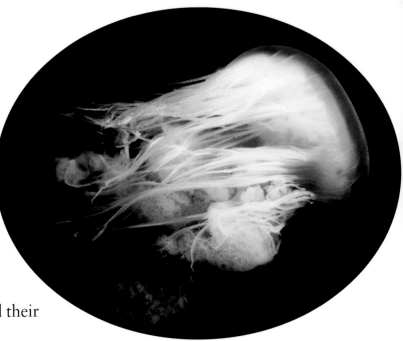

Lion mane jellyfish are named for the thick, wispy appearance of their tentacles.

cnidarian, live in fresh water. They are polyps, but can move by doing somersaults. They bend their bodies, then stand on their tentacles and flip all the way over again.

Watch out for the Portuguese man-o-war! One wrong step and you might be stung.

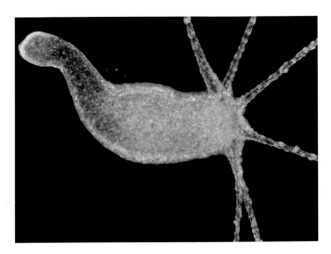

Tiny hydra move by turning somersaults in the water.

A sea slug called a nudibranch (left) feeds on sea anemones (right).

Sea anemones stick out their tentacles to feed and pull them inside their bodies for safety. When the tentacles are out feeding, sea anemones look rather like underwater flowers. They were once mistaken for plants.

Two clownfish share a home in this sea anemone's tentacles.

The possibility of being stung by a cnidarian does not seem to bother some animals. In fact, certain sea turtles snack on jellyfish despite getting swollen eyes from the stings.

Clownfish, small brightly colored fish, hide amid sea anemones' stinging tentacles and are resistant to the stings. They coat their bodies with a slimy substance called mucus, which they mix with the toxin from the anemones' tentacles. As a result, an anemone thinks the clownfish is part of its own body and does not sting it. In return for protection from predators, clownfish clean off algae that grow on the sea anemones. Clownfish and sea anemones live together to help each other survive. This relationship is known as **mutualism**.

Corals

No tropical island paradise is complete without a coral reef lining its coasts. Found in shallow ocean environments, coral reefs are large structures made from the skeletons of millions of tiny coral animals. Reefs are home to a diverse and colorful community of living things.

The feathery tentacles of soft coral provide good hiding places for fish.

Scuba divers and snorkellers enjoy exploring the different kinds of coral found in reefs. Staghorn coral can grow into huge, branching colonies.

A close look at a stony coral colony reveals the six sets of tentacles surrounding the mouth of each individual coral polyp.

Individual corals are tiny polyps, but most grow together in groups called colonies. Each kind of coral colony takes a distinct shape. Brain corals form round, wrinkly colonies. Sea fans form large, branching, fan-shaped colonies.

The reef-building corals are known as "hard," or stony, corals. Each polyp produces a hard skeleton made of calcium carbonate around its body for protection. These skeletons fuse in colonies. As old corals die, new ones grow on top of them, adding their own skeletons. Gradually a reef structure forms consisting of the skeletons of millions of corals.

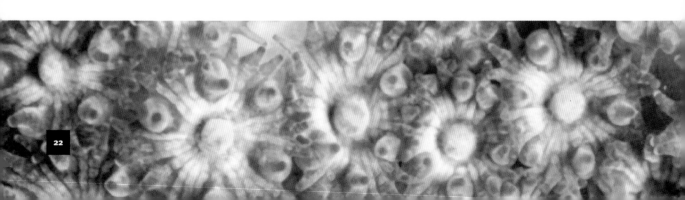

Soft coral sea fans (left) and stony brain coral (right) are found together on a coral reef.

Soft corals usually have eight tentacles surrounding their mouths, while stony corals typically have six. All corals keep their tentacles safely tucked inside their bodies unless they are feeding. Soft corals usually feed during the day, stony corals at night.

Each polyp's skeleton is about the size of a fingernail, so coral reefs grow very slowly. But they can be vast. The Great Barrier Reef off the coast of Australia stretches more than 2,000 kilometers! Reefs can also be very old. Some of today's large reefs have been built up over millions of years.

Not all coral species build reefs. Some, such as sea fans, grow in coral reef environments but do not contribute to the reef-building process. Non-reef-building species are known as "soft" corals, because their sturdy skeletons are not made of calcium carbonate.

Branches of soft coral resemble underwater bushes.

The same coral reef that looked like a hard rock structure during low tide appears to bloom at high tide as each polyp waves its petallike tentacles in the water to feed.

Phylum Platyhelminthes

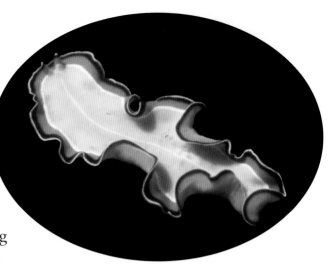

The squirmy, wiggly creatures known as worms vary so widely that they are grouped into several phyla. The simplest belong to the phylum Platyhelminthes, which means "flat worm" in Greek. As you might expect, their bodies are flat, much like a ribbon.

Marine flatworms can be brightly colored with ruffled edges.

Flatworms differ from cnidaria and porifera, because they have a front end (a head), and a back end (a tail). A flatworm's head has eyespots, primitive organs that sense light and dark. They are connected to brainlike organs called **ganglia** that process information received from the eyespots. When the eyespots sense a movement nearby, the flatworm's muscles move the body in response— either toward the movement (if it is food) or away (if it is an enemy).

Scientists think that ancient flatworms were the first animals to develop a front and back body plan. Such an arrangement gives direction and purpose to an animal's movement. For example, the animal can actively search for food rather than wait for food to pass by.

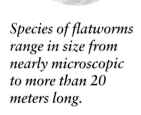

Species of flatworms range in size from nearly microscopic to more than 20 meters long.

Like sponges, flatworms can regenerate their bodies. They reproduce by dividing. If a flatworm's body splits into many pieces, each piece will develop into a new flatworm.

A flatworm has both a head end, with ganglia and eyespots, and a tail end.

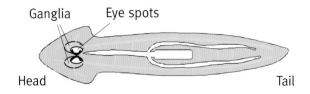

Ganglia   Eye spots

Head   Tail

There are more than 20,000 species of flatworms! Most are parasitic, meaning they live off of other animals. Unlike predators, however, parasites do not kill a host animal to get nourishment from it. One parasite is the tapeworm, which lives in the intestines of cats, dogs, and even in some humans. There it absorbs nutrients from food the host has eaten.

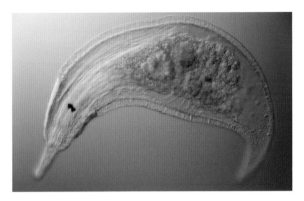

Flatworms stretch and scrunch their bodies in order to move materials from cell to cell.

Many marine flatworms have oval bodies. This one lives on a coral reef.

One kind of non-parasitic flatworm, called **planaria**, is found in fresh water. Planaria are small, scavenging carnivores. **Cilia**, tiny hairlike projections on their undersides, move like oars to push them across logs and rocks in search of food.

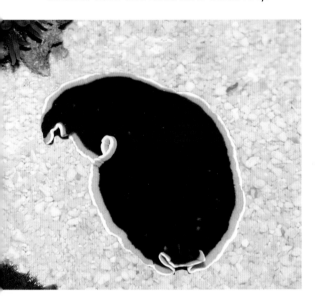

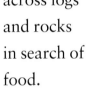

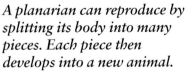

A flatworm moves in purposeful direction— either forward or backward.

A planarian can reproduce by splitting its body into many pieces. Each piece then develops into a new animal.

Phylum Nematoda

Hookworms are parasitic nematodes. These hookworms are feeding on termites.

Roundworms exist wherever water exists—in the ocean, on land, and even on the moist insides of plants and animals. One cup of soil can hold more than a million of them! Some manage to live in extreme environments such as icy glaciers and hot springs.

Roundworms are grouped in the phylum Nematoda, meaning "threadlike" in Greek. They have long, slender, rounded bodies—quite a contrast to the flat bodies of flatworms. Most are so tiny that they are barely visible without a microscope.

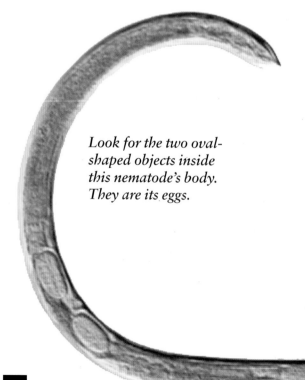

Look for the two oval-shaped objects inside this nematode's body. They are its eggs.

One exception is the parasitic nematode of the sperm whale that can grow up to 13 meters long!

Roundworms have two tiny spots on their heads, but these are not eyespots. Instead, they function as nostrils to smell food and potential enemies. Despite this help, roundworms are not good at escaping predators, because they cannot move very well. Under a microscope, a roundworm looks as if it is thrashing about. It cannot crawl or lift itself. The long muscles running the length of its body make the animal bend from side to side. In the soil, roundworms pull themselves along by bending around soil particles. In the water they just flail around.

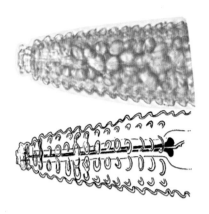 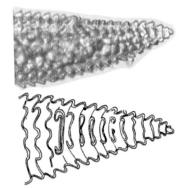

Using a microscope, scientists can study the details inside a nematode's body.

Both the head end and tail end of a nematode's body taper to a point. If you look closely, however, you will see that the head end (top) is slightly thicker than the tail (bottom).

A roundworm's muscles are covered with a skin that produces a tough, flexible protective layer called a **cuticle**. As the worm grows, it sheds its cuticle and regrows a new and bigger one.

Though simple on the outside, nematodes have a complex internal anatomy.

Many roundworms are parasitic. Hookworms, pinworms and intestinal roundworms live inside animals. Others live in plants. Root nematodes, for example, form nodules in the roots of plants that prevent the plant from growing properly. Plant parasite species can cause major diseases in food crops.

Phylum Annelida –
Successful Segments

Earthworms perform an essential ecological function—they plow the soil and recycle nutrients.

Earthworms are called segmented worms because their long bodies are made up of many similar ringlike segments. They are grouped with leeches and bristle worms in the phylum Annelida, which means "little rings" in Latin.

Earthworms breathe through their moist skin.

Annelids range from a couple of millimeters to more than 4 meters long, and can have as many as 200 segments. The annelid body plan is a tube within a tube. The inner tube is the digestive system. It begins at the mouth and ends with the anal slit at the worm's back end. The outer tube is made up of two layers of muscles.

Annelids are covered with a skin that produces a slimy mucus. They actually breathe through their moist skin. If their skin dries out, annelids will suffocate and die.

Earthworms perform an important job in nature—they plow the soil. By burrowing in soil, they create tunnels through which air and water can get to the roots of plants, helping them grow.

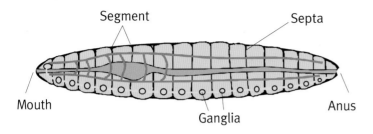

Segment   Septa

Mouth   Ganglia   Anus

Thin sheets of tissue, called septa, separate the segments inside an earthworm. Each segment has a nerve ganglion (plural: ganglia).

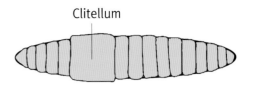

Clitellum

The clitellum, a swelling in the skin of an earthworm, is located close to the front end of a worm's body and is involved in reproduction.

All leeches live in fresh water. They are also called "blood suckers" because many feed on the blood of other animals. They attach to animals with suckers found both on their head and their back end.

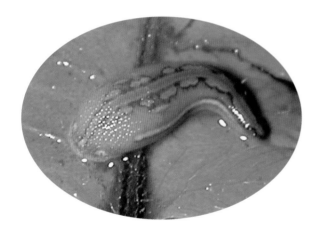

The body of a leech swells when it is full of blood from feeding off a host animal.

Bristle worms get their name from the long, fancy, bristlelike hairs that cover their bodies. They live only in the ocean. Their bristles and bright colors often give them a dramatic appearance.

To move, annelids rely on their muscles. One layer of muscles circles the body in rings. These muscles squeeze the body, making it longer and narrower. The second layer of muscles runs lengthwise along the body. These muscles contract to make the body shorter again. In this way the body moves by lengthening and shortening. The bristles on earthworms and bristle worms and the suckers on leeches grasp the ground as the animals move.

Feather-duster worms, a kind of bristle worm, extend feathery tentacles from their mouths. These tentacles are used in respiration and feeding.

Phylum Mollusca –
The Advantage of a Shell.

It's hard to believe that the snails in a garden, the oysters you eat, and the giant octopuses you see in horror films are all related. Although they look different, they are all grouped in the phylum Mollusca, meaning "soft one" in Latin. All mollusks have soft bodies, a muscular foot for moving and grasping, and a thick skin called a **mantle**. When soft bodies are unprotected, they are easy prey for hungry animals. So the mantle of many mollusks can produce a hard protective outer shell from the calcium carbonate in seawater.

Every seashell you find on the beach once belonged to a mollusk. More than 50,000 species of living mollusks have been identified. The shells of many ancient mollusks have been found as fossils (preserved remains of ancient organisms). Through these fossils, scientists also have a good record of the extinct mollusks— those species which are no longer living.

Background image: On the seafloor, you can find many different kinds of mollusks including snails and clams.

Bivalves

Clams, oysters, and mussels are called **bivalves**, which means "two shells." A muscular hinge connects these two shells so that they can open when an animal wants to feed and close when it wants to protect itself. A bivalve's muscular foot helps it move and anchors it in mud and sand.

The shells of bivalves are connected by a muscular hinge.

Mollusk shells come in a variety of shapes and sizes. The thorny oyster shell is especially vibrant.

Some mollusks use their shell-making ability to cover a sand grain or other particle that gets inside their shells and irritates their soft body. Over time, the particle is covered in many layers of minerals and it becomes a pearl. Oysters are bivalves that produce some of the most highly valued pearls.

Bivalves rarely need to open their shells very wide. They breathe and feed by filtering water through tubes called **siphons** that they push out through even a small opening between the shells. Clams can be fully buried in mud and still breathe and eat by pushing their siphons up out of the seafloor.

The shiny inside of an oyster shell is made of the same material an oyster uses to form pearls.

Gastropods

Snails and slugs are members of the mollusk group known as gastropods, which means "stomach foot." A gastropod's foot is attached to the underside of its belly. Most gastropods carry a spiral-shaped shell on their backs.

Notice the four stalks on a snail's head. The back two are antennae and the front two are eyes.

A shell serves to protect a mollusk's soft body and some gastropod shells are quite beautiful. Brightly colored shells warn potential predators that those gastropods can be toxic if eaten.

A snail moves by extending its head and a muscular foot from its shell.

A snail can pull its entire body inside its shell if it needs to. In fact, most of its body stays inside the shell at all times. When a snail wants to move, however, it has to extend its foot and head out of the shell. The muscles in the foot lengthen and shorten, propelling the animal slowly forward. The foot creates slippery mucus to help it glide over flat surfaces and sticky mucus for climbing. If a snail becomes alarmed, however, it quickly retreats into its shell and plugs the entrance with the hard part of its foot.

Slugs are basically snails without the shell. Although parts of a slug's mantle can be rigid, its soft body is mostly unprotected.

Many gastropods have strikingly beautiful shells.

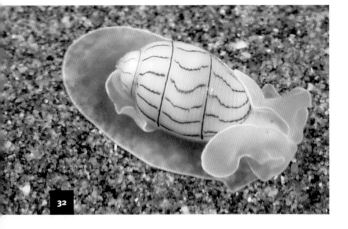

A gastropod's head looks as if it has four antennae. Actually, only two are true antennae, which extend out to sense the animal's surroundings. The other two antennaelike structures are eyes mounted on the ends of stalks.

Many gastropods live on land, more in the water. This orange snail can survive in either environment.

Slugs graze across the forest floor, eating mushrooms and other fungi.

The glowing colors on this toxic nudibranch are a warning to potential predators, "Don't eat!"

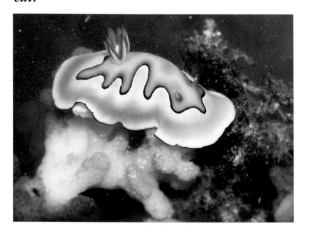

Gastropods have special "tongues," called **radulas,** that are covered in hard, toothlike structures. Radulas can scrape algae off rocks and are strong enough to bore through the shells of prey.

The leopard slug can grow to be more than 15 centimeters long.

Many gastropods live in water. They breathe through gills beneath their shells. Garden snails and slugs are examples of gastropods that live on land. They breathe air through tiny pores in their mantle.

Cephalopods

Some mollusks have learned how to swim. Shells are heavy and difficult to move around, but a long time ago, the nautilus developed the ability to trap air inside its beautiful spiral shell and float. Nautilus shells are also lighter than those of other mollusks, making them quick, successful predators.

Squids have excellent eyesight. Their eyes are located at the back of the head, behind the pen.

The fastest-moving mollusks, the octopus and the squid, no longer produce a shell at all. A rigid structure called a **pen** forms inside a squid's mantle, but an octopus lacks any kind of shelllike structure.

The nautilus, octopus, and squid are **cephalopods**, which means "head foot." The most intelligent of the invertebrates, cephalopods have large brains and can learn and remember. They also have highly developed eyes, which help them to be good hunters. A cephalopod's mouth is shaped like a hard, sharp beak. Like the gastropods, their tongue is a radula.

The mollusk foot has evolved into eight armlike appendages in octopuses and ten such appendages in squid. Each appendage has a row of suction cuplike feet that help to grasp prey. Cephalopods move by a kind of "jet propulsion." That is, they take water into their bodies and then push it out quickly through two siphon tubes on the sides of their bodies. They can also pull themselves along using their arms.

People often collect and cherish beautiful nautilus shells.

The tail end of a squid's mantle has flaps to help guide its movements in the water.

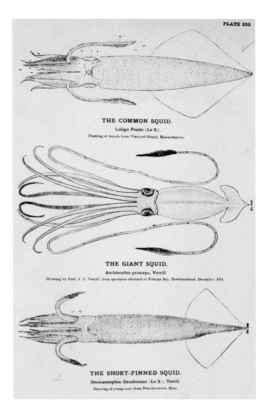

THE COMMON SQUID.
Loligo Pealei (Le S.).
Drawing of female from Vineyard Sound, Massachusetts

THE GIANT SQUID.
Architeuthis princeps, Verrill.
Drawing by Prof. A. E. Verrill, from specimen obtained at Fortune Bay, Newfoundland, December, 1874.

THE SHORT-FINNED SQUID.
Ommastrephes illecebrosus (Le S.), Verrill.
Drawing of young male from Provincetown, Mass.

There are many varieties of squids. The giant squid (center) is the largest of all invertebrates and can grow to be more than 21 meters long.

Although octopuses and squid are hunters, they can be very shy. Squid usually stay in deep, dark waters unless they follow their food to shallower waters. Octopuses hide from enemies by squeezing into the smallest, tightest spaces. When they cannot find a hiding spot, they camouflage their bodies by changing their skin's color and texture to match their background.

When confronting a predator, both squid and octopuses will shoot black ink out of their bodies to distract the predator until they can swim to safety.

Octopuses live in all the oceans, including the muddy deep seafloor.

Phylum Arthropoda

Imagine spending your entire life inside a suit of armor. Animals in the phylum Arthropoda do exactly that. But their armor is not made of metal like that of medieval soldiers. Rather it is made of a lightweight material called chitin that fits perfectly around the soft body of the animal. Unlike the heavy shells of mollusks, arthropod armor, called an **exoskeleton** (outside skeleton), provides protection and also allows for easy movement. People can move because our muscles are attached to our bony skeletons. Arthropods can move because their muscles are attached to their exoskeletons.

Tarantulas can grow to be more than 25 centimeters across (from tip to tip).

Hermit crabs live in the shells of mollusks. When a hermit crab outgrows one shell, it leaves it and looks for another.

"Arthropod" means "jointed foot" in Latin. All these animals have jointed legs and segmented bodies. But that is where their similarity ends. Animals as diverse as butterflies, hermit crabs, tropical centipedes, and tarantulas— more than 80% of all living animal species— belong to the phylum Arthropoda.

Although the name centipede means "hundred-legged," the average centipede has only about 70 legs.

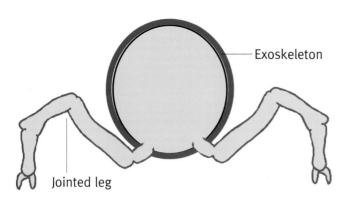

In this cross-section of an arthropod's body, you can see how the exoskeleton covers not only its soft body, but also its jointed legs.

Butterflies, such as the Common Blue above, are also arthropods.

Arthropods are very active animals. Not only do they have a head with a brain to direct their movements, they also have legs to walk, and, in some cases, wings to fly. In some arthropods, legs have developed into specialized appendages for eating, grasping, and sensing.

Ancestors to the modern arthropods are thought to have been some of the first animals to leave the oceans and take up life on land and eventually sky.

Unlike the bones in vertebrate skeletons, exoskeletons do not grow as an animal grows. Rather an animal has to shed its exoskeleton and develop a bigger one as its body grows. This process, called **molting**, occurs when the exoskeleton breaks open, revealing a new, soft skeleton underneath. Once the old skeleton is shed, the arthropod inflates its body to a larger size before allowing the new skeleton to harden.

When arthropods grow too large for their exoskeletons, they molt. Here a tarantula sheds its exoskeleton all in one piece.

Insects

The most abundant and diverse arthropods are insects. All insects, including beetles, butterflies, grasshoppers, and mosquitoes, have three pairs of jointed legs, three body segments (the **head, thorax,** and **abdomen**), and usually have either one or two pairs of wings. Their exoskeletons are very thin and lightweight, which makes flying possible.

The hind legs of a grasshopper are used for jumping. They are much larger than the front two pairs.

Mosquitoes have small bodies and long, delicate legs. The females are parasites and feed on the blood of other animals. Females are also the ones that buzz. Male mosquitoes fly silently and feed on sweet fruit and nectar from flowers.

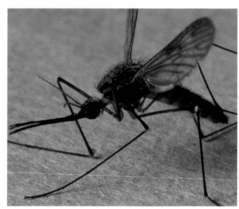

Mosquito antennae are covered in tiny hairs that make them look feathery.

A mosquito pierces the skin of an animal or fruit with its **stylet,** a sharp, hollow mouth part. It then sucks liquid through a strawlike tube called a **proboscis** that projects through the stylet.

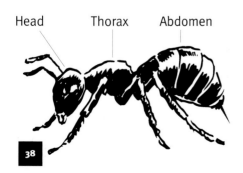

Head   Thorax   Abdomen

An ant has three body sections, three sets of jointed legs, and one pair of antennae— all covered by an exoskeleton.

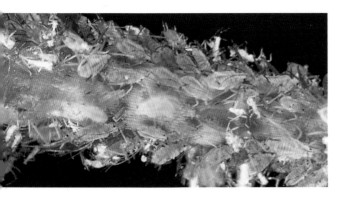

Aphids are tiny insects that live in large colonies on plants. They can eat through an entire rose stem in a very short time.

Grasshoppers have especially large hind legs that enable them to jump. You can often hear grasshoppers "humming" on a summer evening. They make this noise by rubbing their wings together as if they are playing a violin. Many people consider grasshoppers to be pests. They are known to ruin entire crops of food.

People use helpful insects to get rid of pests. Ladybugs are beetles that love to eat aphids, tiny insects known to feed on garden plants.

A caterpillar gorges itself and grows plump. At the right time, it attaches itself to a branch and forms a covering called a chrysalis, around its body. After about a month, a fully formed butterfly breaks out of the chrysalis.

A ladybug's wings are encased under pieces of its exoskeleton. When it gets ready to fly, it lifts its exoskeleton and out come the wings. When it lands, the wings fit neatly back under the exoskeleton. Gardeners collect ladybugs and release them in their gardens to keep their plants free of aphids.

The wings of a ladybug are tucked beneath its red and black exoskeleton.

All insects undergo **metamorphosis**. That is, their bodies change form as they grow from young larvae to adults. Many begin life in lakes and streams and leave the water when they become adults. Perhaps the most dramatic metamorphosis is that of a caterpillar turning into a butterfly.

Lobsters are crustaceans whose front legs have developed into huge, sharp claws.

Other Arthropods

Unlike insects, spiders have two body segments (a **cephalothorax** and an abdomen), eight legs, and typically eight eyes. Small hairs cover the exoskeleton of spiders and help them sense their environment. A special organ called a **spinneret** produces silk

Many tarantulas spin webs that they can hide inside to wait for their prey.

threads, which spiders use to spin intricate webs and to wrap up their eggs and prey. Some spiders are so tiny they are barely visible; others are large enough to cover a person's entire hand.

The flat webs created by orb weavers can be quite intricate.

Millipedes and centipedes have long bodies like worms but with many legs. These long bodies are divided into many armored segments. "Millipede" means "thousand feet." Although they do not really have a thousand feet, each body segment has two pairs of legs. On a long millipede, that can look like a thousand! Centipedes ("hundred feet") have one pair of legs per segment.

Millipedes are scavengers and feed on leaf litter in forests. Their legs make a wavelike movement as they propel the body forward. Centipedes are carnivorous, and their bites can be very poisonous even to humans. They move their bodies in an S-shape.

Crustaceans, including crabs, lobsters and crayfish, are arthropods that mostly live in water. While crustaceans have five pairs of jointed legs, only some of them are used for walking.

A magnified image of a millipede's head shows its segmented antennae.

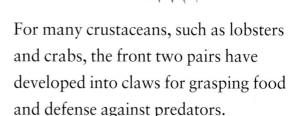

A millipede's exoskeleton covers each of its many segments and bends into a helmetlike layer on the head.

A centipede has one pair of legs for each segment on its long, thin body

For many crustaceans, such as lobsters and crabs, the front two pairs have developed into claws for grasping food and defense against predators.

Crustaceans have two pairs of antennae for sensing the environment. What resembles a third pair of antennae is actually their two eyes. When crabs hide under rocks, they can just stick out their antennae and eyes to sense if there is danger or food nearby.

Rock crabs graze on algae and other food materials they find at the ocean's edge.

Phylum Echinodermata

Sea stars live on coral reefs and feed on corals and mollusks.

Starfish, with their many arms and prickly bodies, are not actually fish. They are better known as sea stars and are grouped with sea urchins, sand dollars, and sea cucumbers in the phylum Echinodermata. The word "echinoderm" means "spiny skin" in Greek. Echinoderms are protected by hard, overlapping plates covered by a thick spiny, skin. They live only in the sea.

Instead of having a head and a tail, the bodies of echinoderms have radial symmetry. That means they have a central body with appendages growing out in every direction like the spokes on a wheel. Most sea stars have five arms, but some can grow many more. The sun star continues to grow new arms throughout its life. Sand dollars and sea urchins do not have appendages, but you can see the radial symmetry in their body shapes.

In each echinoderm, water enters the body through a **madreporite**, a small circular plate that filters out debris. Once inside, water flows through a series of channels throughout the body.

The sun star is named for its sun ray-like appendages.

Top side of a Sea Star

Madreporite

Under side of a Sea Star

Radial canals

Ring canal

Water enters the madreporite on the top side of a brittle sea star's central body. The water is then pumped along canals in the body (orange) to the brittle sea star's many feet on its under side.

Echinoderms have hundreds of tiny suction feet.

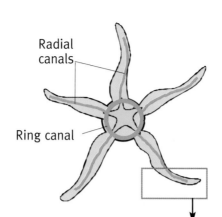

Echinoderms move by pumping water into their feet. The underside of an echinoderm is covered with hundreds of tiny tube feet. When the feet are pumped full of water, they swell, allowing the echinoderm to move. A suction cup on the tip of each foot helps it stick to the surface it is moving across. In a coordinated motion, the tube feet swing forward, hold their place with suction, and then pull the animal forward.

The pattern on the surface of a sand dollar's body shows its radial symmetry.

Sand dollars look rather like large coins. Their spines are much smaller than those on the sea urchins, and these animals usually partially bury themselves in the sand.

Sea urchins are known as the "pincushions" of the sea. Their round bodies are covered in hard, sharp spines that could be mistaken for the pins sticking out of a pincushion.

A sea urchin's spines are long and prickly.

43

Sea Stars

Scientists have identified more than 6,000 species of echinoderms. More than 5,000 of them are sea stars.

Sea stars like to eat corals, mollusks, and other echinoderms. The crown-of-thorns sea stars are known to ravage coral reefs, eating polyp after polyp. Mollusk-eating sea stars have an unusual feeding behavior. They climb on top of a mollusk and use the suction cups on their tube feet to grasp onto and pry open the shell. The mollusk will try to keep its shell shut, but eventually it gets tired. If a sea star can get the shell open even a crack, it pushes its stomach out of its mouth and into the shell. Inside the shell, the sea star's stomach chemicals digest the mollusk's soft body.

Crown-of-thorns sea stars feed on coral. They have eaten entire patches of coral in the Great Barrier Reef during times of high population.

Fishermen who harvest mollusks have to compete with mollusk-eating sea stars. For a long time, whenever these fishermen found a sea star, they would chop it up and throw it back overboard. What they did not know is that this would only make their

Though sunflower stars have plenty of legs, they still regenerate injured ones.

problem worse. Sea stars have the ability to regenerate their bodies, and most of the chopped-up pieces grew into fully developed sea stars. The fishermen were actually multiplying the number of sea stars instead of decreasing them.

Scientists have studied sea stars very closely to understand how regeneration works. They have learned that the central body of the sea star is crucial. If a sea star loses an arm, it will grow a new one. If the arm that broke off has even a few cells from the central body attached to it, it will grow into a new sea star. But if the arm has no part of the central body, it cannot regenerate into a new sea star.

Echinoderms live in all sorts of marine environments from shallow pools to deep oceans.

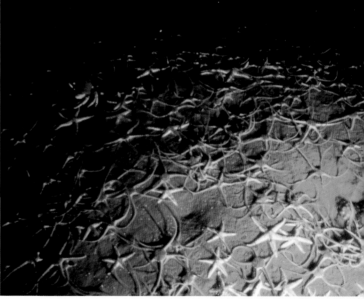

Spiny sea stars, armored arthropods, slimy slugs, beautiful bristleworms, and colonial coral—all are incredible invertebrates!

Glossary

abdomen The rear body section of an arthropod.

animal kingdom One of the main groups into which all living things are divided. Most organisms in the animal kingdom are capable of movement, contain a nervous system, and take in food to produce energy.

Annelida The phylum of invertebrate animals that includes earthworms and all other segmented worms.

Arthropoda The phylum of invertebrate animals, including insects and spiders, with exoskeletons, jointed legs, and segmented bodies. More than 80% of all living animal species are arthropods.

bivalve A mollusk with two shells connected by a hinge. Clams, oysters, and mussels are bivalves.

budding A method of reproduction in which pieces of a sponge break off and develop into new sponges.

cell The basic unit of living things. There are many different types of cells, each with a different job to do.

cephalopod A mollusk that can swim and has appendages attached to its head. Octopuses and squids are cephalopods.

cephalothorax In arachnids, the front section of the body that includes the head.

cilia Tiny, moving, hairlike structures on the bodies of flatworms.

classification The process of dividing things into groups according to their characteristics.

Cnidaria The phylum of aquatic, invertebrate animals that have the ability to sting. Jellyfish and sea anemones are cnidaria.

cuticle The protective layer of skin on a roundworm.

Echinodermata The phylum of aquatic invertebrates protected by a thick, spiny skin. Sea stars, sea urchins, and sand dollars are echinoderms.

exoskeleton The hard, outside body-covering of an arthropod.

flagella Taillike structures on a cell that move back and forth.

ganglion (plural: ganglia) A simple, brainlike organ found in some animals. Many invertebrates have ganglia.

gastropod A mollusk with a foot attached to its underbelly. Most, including snails, have a single spiral shaped shell. Slugs have no shell at all.

head The top or front part of a body.

insects Arthropods with three pairs of jointed legs and three body segments. Most have one or two pairs of wings.

invertebrate An animal without a backbone. Insects and worms are examples of invertebrates.

larva (plural: larvae) The early life stage of certain animals that are not fully developed.

madreporite In an echinoderm, a central body plate full of holes through which water enters the body.

mantle A thick outer covering on a mollusk's body. In some mollusks, the mantle produces a shell.

medusa A body form of cnidaria. Medusae float freely in the water.

metamorphosis The series of changes in body shape that certain animals go through as they develop from eggs to adults.

Mollusca The phylum of invertebrate animals with soft bodies, a muscular foot for movement, and a mantle.

mutualism A relationship between two animals in which both animals benefit.

molt To shed the exoskeleton or skin.

Nematoda The phylum of invertebrate animals that include roundworms.

osculum A large pore through which filtered water leaves the body of a sponge.

ostia (singular, **ostium**) The tiny pores, or holes, on the outer layer of a sponge.

pen A rigid structure inside a squid.

phylum (plural: phyla) A large group of organisms sharing similar characteristics. Phyla are the primary divisions in the animal kingdom.

planaria A nonparasitic flatworm found in fresh water.

Platyhelminthes The phylum of invertebrate animals that includes more than 20,000 species of flat worms.

polyp A body form of cnidaria. A polyp attaches to rocks, shells, or the seafloor by its feet.

Porifera The phylum of the simple, invertebrate animals called sponges.

proboscis A long, hollow tube that is the mouth part of many insects.

radula The tongue of many mollusks which is covered in hard, toothlike structures.

regenerate To grow back or repair parts which have been damaged. In some animals, regeneration is a method of reproduction.

siphon In bivalves, a tube used for breathing and feeding.

species A group of organisms which have many characteristics in common.

spicules Tiny fibers or minerals that make up a sponge's skeleton.

spinneret An organ in some invertebrates, including spiders, that produces silk.

spongin The flexible, skeletal structure of some sponges. The natural sponges people use for cleaning have spongin skeletons.

stylet In mosquitoes, the sheath around the proboscis (see proboscis).

thorax The middle body section of many arthropods.

vertebrate An animal with a backbone and well-developed brain. Mammals, birds, and fish are examples of vertebrates.

Index